Pearl
Harbor

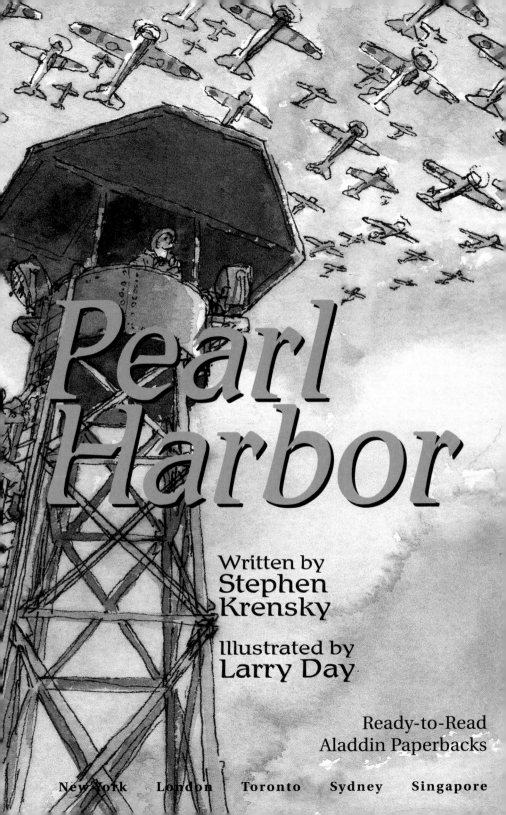

Pearl Harbor

Written by
Stephen Krensky

Illustrated by
Larry Day

Ready-to-Read
Aladdin Paperbacks

New York   London   Toronto   Sydney   Singapore

For Michael

First Aladdin Paperbacks edition May 2001

Text copyright © 2001 by Stephen Krensky
Illustrations copyright © 2001 by Larry Day

Aladdin Paperbacks
An imprint of Simon & Schuster Children's Publishing Division
1230 Avenue of the Americas
New York, NY 10020

The text for this book was set in Utopia.
The illustrations were rendered in watercolor.
Printed and bound in the United States of America

2 4 6 8 10 9 7 5 3

CIP Data for this book is available from the Library of Congress.

ISBN 0-689-84214-7 (Aladdin pbk.)

Table of Contents

A Tense Meeting

The American secretary of state Cordell Hull stood angrily beside his desk. Outside in the hall, two Japanese diplomats had arrived with a letter. It contained the latest answer from Tokyo about Japan's willingness to leave occupied territory in China and Indochina.

On this Sunday, December 7, 1941, Hull had kept the diplomats waiting for fifteen minutes. Now, as they entered, his expression remained grim. The chief envoy, Kichisaburo Nomura, stepped forward, offering to shake hands.

Hull refused—though he had shaken Nomura's hand many times before.

The Japanese government had told the two diplomats to deliver the letter at 1:00 P.M. But they had been delayed more than an hour decoding and copying it.

In that hour the world had changed.

As Nomura gave the letter to Hull, he glanced at it briefly. Then he threw it down on his desk. Hull knew exactly what the document contained. American cryptographers had broken the Japanese code the year before, and

he had already received a copy of its contents.

But none of that mattered now. The paper, he told them, was filled with "infamous falsehoods." Clearly, Japan had no intention of giving up any land in China.

The Japanese didn't know what to say—and in any case, Hull was in no mood to listen. With a wave of his hand, he ordered them out.

"Scoundrels!" he muttered. The confused diplomats did not yet know

the news that Hull himself had just learned. Japan, while pretending to show interest in peaceful solutions, had been secretly preparing for war at that moment. And unknown to Hull, the attack had already begun.

A Shadow Grows

Three months earlier, the fall of 1941 had started much like any other. The leaves had changed color. The birds had flown south. And the New York Yankees had won the World Series.

At the White House, however, President Franklin D. Roosevelt had little time to think about sports or the weather. He was too busy keeping track of changing events around the world.

The news abroad was bad and getting worse. Europe had been at war for two years. The forces of Nazi Germany had already defeated many countries, from Poland in the East to France in the West. Great Britain still fought on, but her cities had been bombed and her defenses were weakening. "We shall

fight in the fields and in the streets," Prime Minister Winston Churchill had declared, "we shall fight in the hills; we shall never surrender."

While Churchill rallied the British people, war also loomed across the Pacific. For years the Empire of Japan

had steadily expanded its influence in the Far East. And now Japanese ships and troops were moving to strategic locations throughout Southeast Asia.

So far the United States remained at peace. President Roosevelt tried to make it clear that the United States could not afford to just sit back and watch. The war in Europe, he explained, was like a fire at a neighbor's house. If the neighbor "can take my garden hose and connect it up with his hydrant," he said, "I may help him to put out the fire." And if that fire is extinguished, the president went on, the whole neighborhood may be saved from going up in flames.

Still, America was officially neutral. It was not just a question of choosing between right and wrong. The country was still recovering from hard times. The nation's army and navy were also in poor shape. There were not enough soldiers to fight or guns and ships to fight with. Young men were still enlisting, getting physicals, and being trained for combat. But their numbers were limited. In 1940, there were 190,000 American soldiers compared to 320,000 in Japan and 800,000 in Germany. Before challenging these forces, America had a lot of catching up to do.

At such a time, predicting the future
was almost impossible. But one thing
was clear. The United States was not
ready to jump into a war on its own.

The War Machine

For Japan, the war in Europe appeared as a special opportunity. France, Holland, and Great Britain each had valuable Asian colonies producing rice, oil, or rubber. For the Japanese, who relied on other countries for many raw materials, capturing these prizes was a tempting prospect.

Until the mid-nineteenth century, Japan had largely kept apart from the rest of the world. But after the American commodore Matthew Perry forced Japan to open up for trade in 1853, Western science and invention had followed. And the natural resources that those inventions required had helped to fuel the

Japanese quest for expansion.

But before the Japanese could begin leapfrogging across the Pacific, they had to deal with the United States. As an ally of the European countries, the United States would not stand around while the Japanese swallowed up one European colony after another.

Some Japanese leaders, however, were not worried about the United States. They thought Americans were soft and aimless. They would not have the spirit to fight a lengthy war that did not threaten their homeland.

But the head of the Japanese navy, Admiral Isoroku Yamamoto, disagreed. He was well aware of the country's industrial strength. America might seem like a slumbering giant, but he was hesitant to wake it up.

Therefore, if the Japanese government insisted on war, Yamamoto thought there was only one way to win it. A first strike against the United States must be planned, a strike so crippling that America would not recover for a long time.

The strike itself would not signal the first step in an invasion. Conquering the United States was not a Japanese goal. Japan wanted something simpler: to gain enough time to secure other Pacific conquests. Would Americans choose to fight and die halfway around the world to save people and places that most of them could never find on a map?

Yamamoto didn't think so.

By October of 1941, pressures were building in the Japanese government to take action. Already, the United States, Great Britain, and the Netherlands together had cut off Japan from all sources of imported oil. Without oil, Japan certainly could not fight a war, but it also could not survive in peace. Japan had to act before its resources ran out.

Japan also had a new prime minister

and military leader—General Hideki Tojo. While the Emperor Hirohito was Japan's supreme ruler, General Tojo wielded a great deal of power. The army was eager for war, and the Empire of Japan had not been defeated in more than one thousand years.

Morning at Pearl Harbor

As dawn broke on the morning of December 7, William Outerbridge stood aboard the destroyer *U.S.S. Ward*. The *Ward* was patrolling the waters off Hawaii, and Outerbridge was scanning the ocean for anything out of the ordinary.

Suddenly he caught sight of a submarine heading toward Pearl Harbor. No friendly ship had any business being in such a place, and Outerbridge ordered the *Ward*'s guns to open fire. When the sub's conning tower was hit at 6:54 A.M., the submarine submerged. Soon the *Ward* spotted another submarine and fired depth charges against it.

Shortly before 7:00 A.M., soldiers at an army radar station on Oahu noted a large blip on the screen. At first, the soldiers on duty thought the equipment was malfunctioning. But after checking it over, they reported the sighting.

News of both incidents made its way to military headquarters, but neither incident drew much attention. No American or British officials expected Japan to directly attack the United States. Hawaii and the American mainland, they thought, were too far from

the territories the Japanese wanted to be likely targets.

Sadly, they were mistaken. A Japanese strike force—six aircraft carriers with supporting battleships and cruisers—had sailed from Japan on November 25. Hoping to escape detection, the fleet had kept to stormy seas 275 miles north of Hawaii. American radio operators detected low-frequency communications coming from the area. Unfortunately, no one investigated the matter.

From that unsettled patch of ocean, more than three hundred bombers and

fighters were launched in two waves before and after dawn on December 7.

Several hours passed before the Japanese planes, which had been flying at 9,800 feet, broke through the cloud cover. Although the Japanese still hoped for a surprise attack, they were not counting on it.

But Commander Mitsuo Fuchida, leader of the Japanese forces, found the skies empty. No one was stirring, no defense was waiting for him.

Celebrating his good fortune, he radioed the order to attack.

"Tora! Tora! Tora!"

Down on the ground, long lines of

servicemen were waiting for breakfast. Others were in the cabins aboard their ships, wrapping Christmas presents to be mailed home that week. The unexpected rumble of planes overhead drew curious glances, but no one realized the danger until the Japanese Zeros flew in and began firing their machine guns.

The bombs began falling at 7:55 A.M. By 8:25 A.M., the first waves of torpedoes

and dive-bombers struck. Ninety-six American ships sat in the harbor, including all eight battleships of the Pacific fleet. They bobbed there like ducks in a barrel, unable to move and unprepared to fight back.

On the *Arizona,* the bombs hit the forward turret and blew a hole in the

boiler beneath. The sudden explosion rocked the ship, killing one thousand men before they even knew the air-raid alarms had sounded.

A wall of fire engulfed the *Tennessee,* and five torpedoes scuttled the *Oklahoma.* The *Maryland, West Virginia,* and *California* were soon heavily damaged. The *Nevada* was crippled as she

tried to head out to sea. Only the *Pennsylvania,* undergoing repairs in a dry dock, was less heavily hit.

As the battleships came under fire, crewmen tried to jump into the water and swim to safety. A thick slick of oil was gushing from the damaged ships

and burning across the water. Many of the sailors never made it to shore.

At Wheeler and Hickam Air Fields, the Japanese destroyed hundreds of parked planes. They were all huddled

together wingtip-to-wingtip, which made them easier to guard from island-based sabotage. Unfortunately, it also made them easier to destroy from the air.

At 8:40 A.M., the second wave of Japanese planes crossed Oahu. Standing in his office, Admiral Husband E. Kimmel, commander of the fleet, watched in horror as the destruction unfolded.

Suddenly a spent bullet shattered a window. It bounced harmlessly off the admiral's chest before falling to the floor. Kimmel looked at the bullet in disgust. "Too bad it didn't kill me," he said quietly.

By 10:00 A.M., the battle was over. Dazed crewmen searched for lost friends in the burning waters and leveled buildings. The Zeros were gone as quickly as they had come, leaving behind pillars of smoke and fire that burned long into the day and night.

War and Peace

"Yesterday," President Roosevelt said solemnly, "December 7, 1941—a date which will live in infamy—the United States of America was suddenly and deliberately attacked by naval and air forces of the Empire of Japan."

So began the president's message to the United States Congress. The news of Pearl Harbor had swept across the

country with hurricane force, leaving both horror and disbelief in its path.

"No matter how long it may take us to overcome this premeditated invasion," said the president, "the American people in their righteous might will win through to absolute victory."

These were brave words. But neither Roosevelt nor anyone else underestimated the struggle ahead. The

losses, after all, had been horrible: 2,330 servicemen and 100 civilians were dead. Another 2,000 were wounded. All 8 American battleships had been sunk or crippled. And 188 aircraft had been destroyed on the ground.

The Japanese had also struck the British in Malaya and Hong Kong, and American bases in the Philippines and other islands.

There was some good news. Pearl Harbor's dockyard facilities and oil stores were unharmed. Most importantly, the two American aircraft carriers *Enterprise* and *Lexington* were still safely out at sea. Had they been destroyed as well, the Japanese victory might well have been complete.

Even so, the Japanese now controlled the Pacific. Both Admiral Yamamoto and Emperor Hirohito believed their mission had been a success. With

American forces so deeply wounded, they would never recover in time to challenge the Japanese advances.

They were wrong. Thousands swarmed into military recruiting offices to enlist.

Congress immediately declared war on Japan. Three days later, Nazi Germany, Japan's ally, declared war on the United States. During the dark

months that followed, the cry of "Pearl Harbor!" echoed throughout the land.

The war finally ended in 1945. But the war's end did not mean forgetting about the sneak attack. Pearl Harbor remains a symbol of a time and a place when the country ignored an all-too-present danger. Today a memorial marks the spot above the still-sunken *Arizona*. It is both a hope and a reminder that such an event should never happen again.